SWAN FEAST

SWAN FEAST

NATALIE EILBERT

Swan Feast

19 18 17 16 15 1 2 3 4 5
Second Edition

Design & composition: Shanna Compton, shannacompton.com
Cover collage: Jasmine Golestaneh, jasminegolestaneh.tumblr.com
Author photo: Emily Raw, emilyraw.com
Proofreading for first edition: Monroe Hammond

Published by Bloof Books
www.bloofbooks.com
New Jersey

Bloof Books are printed in the USA by Bookmobile and Spencer Printing. Booksellers, libraries, and other institutions may order direct from us by contacting sales@bloofbooks.com. POD copies are distributed via Ingram, Baker & Taylor, and other wholesalers. Individuals may purchase our books direct from our website, from online retailers such as Amazon.com, or request them from their favorite bookstores.

Please support your local independent bookseller whenever possible.

ISBN-13: 978-0-9826587-9-6
ISBN-10: 0-9826587-9-6

1. American poetry—21st century. 2. Poets, American—21st century.

♾ This paper meets the requirements of ANSI/NISO Z39.48-1992

For Dolan Morgan

CONTENTS

11 —With Queen of Willendorf

ONE

13 The Death & Life of the Venus City

TWO

25 Venus of Anorexia
26 [letter excavated from the willendorf tomb]
27 Epithalamium
28 The Husbands of Willendorf
29 First Conjecture of the Venus Figurine
30 Bee Lullaby
31 Supplication with the Venus Figurine
33 The Willendorf Wife
34 With Dead Brother in the Venus Landscape
35 Retouching the Venus Figurine with Focus on Torso
36 The Venus Figurine as It Relates to Gnosticism
37 Homecoming with the Venus Figurine
38 Inheriting the Paleolithic Art Anthology
39 First Conjecture of the Self with Figurine
40 We Watch as If Waiting for the Artifact to Open Her Eyes.

THREE

43 Conversation with the Stone Wife

FOUR

53 [letter excavated from the willendorf tomb]
54 Note Torn from the Wife-Book after the Storm
55 Northeast of Aruba
56 I Want a Love
57 Consider a Landscape
59 Imprecation
61 Epithalamium

62 [letter excavated from the willendorf tomb]
63 Old Wives' Tale
64 Epithalamium
65 Galaxy Meat
67 I Had Grand Notions of the Pasture
68 Inventing the Etymology of My Newest Country
70 Epithalamium
71 Swan Meat
72 [letter excavated from the willendorf tomb]

FIVE

73 The Death & Life of the Venus City
75 On the Confrontation with Men & History
77 How Hunger, How Horse
79 That Special Someone
80 Peak Shift Effect
82 Dr. Szombathy Receives Our Letter
84 In the Mood for Love
86 (The Morning Oils Stain Behind My Nails)
88 Wedding Registry
89 What Doom?

SIX

93 Chiaroscuro

97 Notes
98 Acknowledgments
99 About the Author
100 Praise for *Swan Feast*

"The female representations seem to be some of the most ancient in the entire world, and the statuettes known as the Venus of Willendorf, in Austria, and the Venus of Grimaldi, in Italy . . . number among the most beautiful and noble religious objects relating to the universal Great Mother."

—from Jean Markale's *The Great Goddess*

Tracy Lord: "How do I look?"
Seth Lord: "Like a Queen. Like a Goddess."
Tracy Lord: "And do you know how I feel?"
Seth Lord: "How?"
Tracy Lord: "Like a human. Like a human being."

—*The Philadelphia Story*

"I love these sweet doomed people." —The Venus of Willendorf

—WITH QUEEN OF WILLENDORF

I am not about to go to Texas but I do love that dress.
In my dead times I lived between my waist and a string.
I have never sunbathed on the hood of a car even.
Even though I lived in a trailer and trailer girls have had their asses on hoods.
I have my very own origin story would you like to hear it.
Men have traveled over mountains to listen to my songs.
They have latched their karabiners to my thighs and pulled me close, my sob story closer.
I shared a first period with the kitten I found and loved under the porch when I was ten.
I followed her mewl to her bright red spot, she followed my catcalls to mine.
My best friend was a fatty named the Venus of Willendorf.
She was too heavy to be invisible, and so they let her in.
She asked me what it felt like that my thighs never touched.
I didn't tell her that the mountain men could hear me, that they were still here.
I said like nothing, air moving terrific inside the great lungs of an ice climber.
I wanted this voice to be different.
I wanted this voice to be like a crown spinning on marble floors.
I wanted this voice to be like nothing at all.
I couldn't wear my own throat.
I could wear the throats of others like the highways of America.
The highways of America wear too many throats, in my opinion.
I bend down to be closer to the legs of a chair, to her braided head.
That dumb misguided tension between my legs is still there.
Hello, Venus. Hello, queens.
One day I wake up and I am a woman.
Womanhood is that pushing on your sacrum, a pain which softens to pink-white static.
I picked a job as a salesman and died a wealthy man on a deathbed of slogans.
Where will you spend all eternity, one pamphlet demands.
V clubbed her ears with a spoon but otherwise stood in that eternity spending her time.
When I died I skipped home to tell her about it, no taste of mountains in my mouth.

1

THE DEATH & LIFE OF THE VENUS CITY

I am sick of drawing this connection: there is no document
of civilization that isn't also its ruins. Ask for rapture, get a god.
Ask for Venus, private stones winter underground.
Today I am vain enough in my commute
to peak my reflection in the train window,
overhear a man say You can tell the pretty ones from the ugly
under subway lights. My face mobs between plexiglas,
my anger where the dark face of my queen turns away.
See also a woman's age hidden in her hands,
the veins' bubonic ghosts. For Venus, I wish only our beautiful women
dead and scattered beneath the earth, decently, decently.

The Venus of Willendorf was found
in 1908, a leap year, the same year oil was found in the Middle East.
The archaeologist called her *Venus* but there is nothing Western
about the mounds of genitals, the faceless bravery of womanhood
there caked with a silt called *loess* meaning loose.
See then the man turning her over to dust time loose
from her breast. Mundane artifacts litter the streets, they make
a country's gradients a flag I'll dare its spitted grounds to worship.

A sick woman over her cart now bites her lips into white ash
and I want to declare ourselves a company of women below the earth,
but, dear city, know so help me I won't help her stand for her stop.
As the Venus was nothing but stone, I won't even look in her eyes.
At what age does a woman's body become
the insult of a woman's body. In answer, my hands crack another year
and I sit bored. I want to stand plain here until bled out, but don't.
I am just another punctual slave abandoned by her queen.
Man is free until he wakes, when time returns with the drama
of throwing an ether vial into the flames.
The document of civilization digitized and on the clock
Wednesday Thursday Friday without relief
or dignity, the Venus of Willendorf's document clean as a third-degree burn.

◆ ◆ ◆

No I'll resist the urge to see myself walking in the building glass.
I'm vain in a hurry my youth is fading and earth it isn't sad
earth has no name as Venus has no name. I cross the street,
the heat of trucks wish me dead. If the space in my office
could spread just an inch my joy would tear every curtain of this city down.
In every scene, I am always the handsome spectator delighting
in the spectacle to delight in himself, time a dumb glass eye.
But what I want is Venus, my vision of thrones
and queenless moors, the heathering iceland where she was conceived, mothered
to stone and dirt. So go our desires. Our flesh dares us be bovine, I'll starve it out
to wear it like the cloth of a flag, an allegiance founded
in the vinegar bruise on an arm.

The city sun sets every day now like Muybridge's horse, suffering time.

I think of her creation when I sit in my office,
when my hands rhythmically knot and unknot my hair
and I am the image of a network of thoughts always about to happen.
You see it isn't her art that confounds us but the hands the body
of men if they were eager to make her, was it divine inspiration or
was it boredom, the cold literature of Europe's ice age, boredom
likewise in the flesh of the survivor, boredom which serves to end us
with desired relief. Could they see no errand in the snow, no ramshackle
beauty in death. How else to express the air as harsh, the women as willing,
the earth a delicate dish for their plastic and shit. Her purpose
was her mimesis of riches, the fat breasts like our towers:
without owning them their sight provides a propriety still.
This sick glint of empire bores me of empire.
In this city of boredom, how blankly everything is mine.

◈ ◈ ◈

What will amount to our kingdoms, our Willendorf in the sand.
Can I speak for the Venus, alien object, the way one walks
over seeds buried loose in the snow, can I speak for her
the way a grave-good decorates a ritual, the way styrofoam brims
laughably in the municipal trash. I will speak for her as I spoke
for myself as a girl behind her bedroom door. When I found her
she was marked in Grandpa Leo's anthology an ugly thing to watch:
in her image the hands still combed her form, a log against nothing.

I'll quit the Venus to invent this place: the city's conspired eternity
false, the doomed sensation of unwrapping soft high-fructose
pastry false. As a pigeon lights in bramble attempting a nature,
her discovery galvanized us, gave us the potentiated
human as participant and prophet Monday Tuesday Wednesday—
her brute bauble of god, of slut and man, her hue and cry saved
to my browser history Monday Tuesday Wednesday. Man would be
the ruin of his choice like a city inspecting itself to minimize the damage
of unforeseen calamities like a man turning her over to theorize
origins, her non-diegetic tooth and war, the pain I presume her
to possess in her fissures see since pain is a woman's only natural
possession. What, forsooth, could I know of the Venus body, belly obsessed,
running its dumb country into the ground. Do you see the very falsehood
—no. No, man wears his hubris like an invisible hat, like a single feather
in the snow: we want to belong without question to solution, ha!
With hilarious privilege I watch a man I never loved disappear in the silt.

◆ ◆ ◆

The death and life of great American cities is about negotiating
influences and the impression of citizens, according to Jane Jacobs.
I try to remember the last time I said the word *tribe* without irony,
without the ballast of guilt and privilege that begets my America.
A city is not a work of art, it does not show our humanity nor can it
represent its own artifact though its petroleum suns on my shoulders
wait to banish us. See I'll place the invention of city over the figurine:
whether out of idleness or expression, she was formed but could never
stand upright, she was the anti-city in her impractical mobility: no man
could enter her. I had a city when the harbor lifted, when the tunnels
collapsed and became my dirty sky. I could claim proof of residency,
I could set conditions for my city's diversity based on my size and zoning laws.

The figurine fused to my joints, I imagine myself an incredible
bone artist millennia from now when I'm dug up,
polished, and set again. Discovery renders
archaeologists sole creators of their artifacts, just as man is sole creator
of man. So history says I am meat until discovery makes my importance nameless.
The people then will they see the pride of their
creations further established in these bones of mine, will text read
as nonsense, should I consider the importance of my own longevity
enough to stop drinking. In my Venus city, I will bury the burning lights,
roost over what is left of dirt to seed. I go home and I go home.
I read my queen from the couch to the bed,
her absence like a freezer door left open in the night, the cold touching
even the moon's dead holes. This idea that we can survive the air
coming down from the city, step over crude development planning
without seeing it, the homeless barely tucked in the avenue
fissures, dust of our loss, means we can be both the animal and what kills it.

◈ ◈ ◈

All night the city flickers Plath's fevers. We can think
of this moment as a sign of dumb calm, the city a kind of
silhouette portrait in which we recognize a past, the future
subject to an artifice we can't as yet conceive. I keep
making the switch from *it* to *she* when addressing the Venus.
It's not that she was ever human but at some point her form
became her fiction—what Jacobs would call the self-destruction
of a city, the relentless competition of a space until its primary
economic function becomes the loss of its function. In this sense
I am lost if the Venus is more art than stone. I have laid out my markets,
these lyric schematics, I wanted to draft and redraft the very function
of her lump kind on my psyche, what it meant to call her mine,
what it meant to own a thing without the debt collectors getting wind
and waiting with a stranger's ease at my door. I should starve
my limbs more, I should be a new exaggeration too like my little bitch god.

My grandmother became too sick to horde the corners of her enormous life,
so I inherited her writing desk, her books (a first edition of *The Old Man
and the Sea*), and the whole ocean's floor of my grandfather's life
though I never met him past my cow-eyed infancy. His textbooks
so outdated science sounded like gossip, the world then loosed to clouds
of American cumulus, an altogether remote land that reveals the fears
of our surfaceless, still-undocumented ends. In the pages the Venus stood
ugly therefore forgettable like the cold remains of an uneaten meal,
like a city I visited once and never again where
not even the dinner plates were warm. Hard to say what brought me back.

◈ ◈ ◈

My heart was broken over a man, I should say I was what he spat out
when he was done chewing the trash of my body. My days were occupied
with nothing but writing Venus poems, a necessary way to escape
the politics of addressing the I. Rather, the politics I wanted to be there
but weren't but were again when I considered the gulf between
tour de force and melodrama had a good deal to do with the male and
female experience: to think there could be an exact anguish, a certain stone
dug up and carved and set again in the dirt. The I should be so nameless
in any work I say as I load and cock the gun. I'm through as the metal
cold against a man's throat, daddy daddy scuttling across silent seas *through*.
There is drama in every construction. It's useless, a rat's last breath.
Diversity is achieved with greater success in larger cities because quite simply

more can be done. I start to imagine the Venus of Willendorf in terms of
aesthetic scale: today a woman decorates her house and incorporates African
masks to give the space a pan-cultural design and no one thinks to stop this.
The Venus is about four inches in height, and I think a mistake in thinking
of her now is the impulse to consider her beauty. We see a naked torso
of a woman and think to worship it, but it isn't *worship* what we're doing
we're checking emails we're responding we're filing resignations into the dirt.
The parts still segmented, zoned, a distance grows out of a distance when the body
is warped and frozen this way. What was beauty for the people who lived
nowhere, what could beauty do with the enormity of snow. I see the seeds
impossible, uncurling their greens for want of nothing below and above the ice.

◆ ◆ ◆

In love, my body diminishes beautifully. When my skin was a dead moth's wing,
hair fell out in chunks. The *I* became a joke to write about steeped as I was in
declension. I was sorry to be in love with a man made of silt. Back to my hands
they weren't mine they looked aged, the sick skin of mule.
Charles Olson said once to love the world and stay inside it. In the fumes
of loss the Venus city rises out of the sand so that when I was a camel when
time was the infinite desert I didn't move to drink. The lion ages in me still.
This is my inventory, the world. Each day I pack and unpack my objects, subway
cars, elevators, windows, steel, coffee cups, each wrapped in greased pelts,
wi-fi connection like disseminating seeds in snow, brideless marching citizens.
The city like the phenomenon of color is there and I bless the sun for its ability

to hurt us, to stare into an invention like the angry god in wait sharpening its killing
knives in the kitchen sink. I had a city when I dug the Venus out of my anthology,
when her brute angel rose like a crippled hand in the subway fluorescence
and I could say I loved nothing, my form was a medicine I took at the edge
of a lake. Venus was my wife I stayed inside her and the towers
they were connubial steel, forms were the quiet shapes behind closed eyes
I dripped and bled to touch, a way to say *I was part of this*.
To Olson, art is borne out of love: what remains is the city's function,
what can't be displayed only lived inside: consumed and marveling
whatever pastries are left in the landscape of oblivion. I take the Venus
like a doomed man clasps an amulet. The skyscrapers write their odes
to a distant village. In their glint there are chains unmoving
where our beautiful dead women won't return to her wilderness.

2

VENUS OF ANOREXIA

No one said immortality would be easy. I know
for I collect swine for pageantry.

You can't spell profit without thin wrists,

fortune without plaguing the terrarium.

I'm a smeller you know, that's what I am—

You were always right to fear me.
Alien merchants nibble inside me like faun
on my worried organ gardens. The pigs guffaw

as I finish this chapter on the benefits of
May bellies stock and I wonder what limb

isn't delicate enough to be meat this time.

I can train my hunger to do anything, and it listens.
My hunger a fertility goddess rising
under a calcium balm to son and son forever.

Trace my desires on a bonemap; I am yours.
There is nothing but air between my thighs.

[letter excavated from the willendorf tomb]

Madness, *N*, was always there. Just think: inside you I am always an Austrian spring. I invented a city of rabid cats, sucked hard on every nail before its assembly of parts was anything but flotsam and foam. My dear relatives, *N*, they can't appreciate my taste for semen, the moony tang of pleasure, they can't appreciate how godly I'll be, hair grazing thighs grazing towers grazing tit-heavy clouds. *N*, I took the fiberglass in my mouth and bit down, and, *N*, I wanted to insulate and poison this body that made me to suck and taste and god there. There were bricks everywhere, I made them too to graze in the sick like decultured pigeons. And the factories, what more can be said of factories but the word *factory*, I'm in the center of a chemical rainstorm, naked as stone, legs smoother than the mirrors laid down for the birthday cocaine. A human face will press against its glass drugged and ready to lose its dimensions. But I'm a wife tonight. My lap laid down with gingham and wait, I said *N*, don't you dare find me right now in this room. Don't you even dare.

EPITHALAMIUM

It's true that we were meant
to live in the woods but the day
is not over yet I'm carrying
this wet death in my mouth to you.
It has been centuries since
you've shown me your teeth,
the bald human moment
that cursed your days.
The slick fuck of a couch
in the god-room, of course
the dark entered us. We left
that night, the lake sent for us,
what lake would have us now.
A millennium dawdled out
your perfect dirt scalp, I grew
from the leaves I fell to nothing,
I waited for my very own city
of rust to form edges so
I could form edges. Each hour
you cool in my pocket
is an hour is an hour gone.
See how a journey frames
my lashes, see how I lack
a creation myth, V, an aluminum
sun in the back of my throat.
You pitch the minute to me:
what I own is the damage
of your theorized life. A door
flattening the understory.
I will only speak to you
with closed eyes. The woods
rattle with obsolete rapture.
I live in a nearby shape.

THE HUSBANDS OF WILLENDORF

Years ago they entered my room on horseback, their speech
like their medallions, heavy on their necks, a dark providence.

In a gunnysack I was carried. A dream of the figurine
woke inside me and I swear I felt a horse close its jaws

for good. I knew winter for its stench of clouds, its welcome
blindfold and gag. Wind was not to blame for the rattling door

the nameless house of betrothal. I was bride to the flies,
the Venus stone a cold baguette on a marble slab:

I refused ration. Tomorrow's winter, a document
in a chain of corporate threats. The figurine like a page

torn from the god diary, we received its foul monopoly
of image. No scripture was mentioned. A boy paddled

his kayak to a lake edge to be wed, the German sky
stood post and warned *A country is made out of too many childhoods*

to share a history. Venus of nowhere claimed. An army pounded
the earth and I smelled oil, I smelled her dirt, I smelled fists

numinous as warped violins. Time is what ants disappear
into with their leaf mulch. Nothing returns without our sharpened tools.

FIRST CONJECTURE OF THE VENUS FIGURINE

For days I repeated a proverb about poverty and thieves.
At night I would mouth the words for all the songs never

written in my most golden voice. I ate food from my palm
gargoyle-crouched over a familiar ledge. My feet cramped

for so long vines convulsed and tangled inside my toes,
around my ankles like a gilt, but I wouldn't move.

Heard a man fall in love with my form, then forgot. If it was
difficult for me to stay here I think of the city that failed you.

City of legs pushing back, city of miscarriages, city of
leopards waiting in trees for our young. No city, but a dream

of tools for the felled beasts, a *how to remove its flank*
and raise an empire. There was your body a fragment

of shadows. There was your body its mist of ruminant,
the immaculate cud, the old stone hour beginning us.

Horses opened their skin for the flies, hatching out a stream.

BEE LULLABY

Sound said to dictate so I dictate. Sound said there are machines here that want us
to be kind and gone. The phone it rang itself defunct in my dream where a man was

said to hurt me. Outside the highway steams, exhaust wind scarves itself in my blood
like pills since expired. Outside the engines idle not unkind—there is work to be done,

there is a man whose role it is to whisper to my eyelids their decay and I love him.
There is talk of a crashing system. What system. Search engines give you the results

you do and do not need. Pick what is left of the end of days and you will find there is
plenty still to cry about. There are machines here that want us to be kind and gone.

The time I couldn't worry enough to change the sheets, clean the tongue sitting dumb
yet leonine just within me. The trains they make the landscape plain and gullible, they say

there is one city. Imagine then rats, dredged gardens, a cadmium shoreline. The city then,
an assassination of invisible things, the grass intractable yet always sick. I want this

lonesome sun to never leave but each day it takes out a dead man's letters and
folds them again unread. I know how to wake again and again: sound of gradient

winds or static or the constant daughter's skulking shadow. There are machines here
that want us and want us and want us and I do not sleep out of kindness of that want.

SUPPLICATION WITH THE VENUS FIGURINE

The rupture of our little red lives, *V.*
Should I name blames when I say the sun

when it hits the floorboards right here

pushes a lonesome into the tip of my finger,

pushes my mother off a ledge so she is the city

I worship with $4 coffees. I'm late again
and will cancel the therapy I need to not starve

and feel good about starving because lately

your gut is a ballast. My navel smiles deeply
in the folds as I round my back for rabbit's pose.

It's true I've refused to leave the studio until
I can watch my ribs trace their course to my spine.

College Boyfriend #1 taped us fucking once and remarked
later of my terrible thinness. I loved him only then.

It's true I've stared at my breasts long enough

in the bathtub until their fatty geographies

become something other than what they are.

I live and we live in a form uncarved, and so
we lack a mystery. In the long hours between

your creation and my writing this, I called you

inviolable, my bellicose buttercream, the language
teetering into appellation and epithet.

I drank all the myths down, tasted their sinus blood,
and *V*, you are better than these muscle tales—

I can trace a line between us and climb forever

this frictionless unscripted tree. My limbs

virgin and flesh against your dirt, its harrowing dress.

I crave your calm, which like language I can't claim.

Ugly one, your gaze is only as dead as your gaze.

THE WILLENDORF WIFE

What you're feeling is the need to define
this city and its dependences on effigies and figurines.

Choose the symbol that best describes your reservations
of such a task and burn it. Burn the horse-leather and boars-hair brush

for good measure. At the end of a fortnight, consider the city's
inscrutable need to work in twos; consider the mountaineer's myth

of the goddess encased in rock and the climbers who hump
and strain and slip from the mountain's wet edges.

The phenomenon isn't they dream up the same woman,
not her kohl skin, not her absolute hairlessness—it's the mountain

shifts its face east in the night, its face almost grotesque,
the underside of a firefly stiff on a pane at dusk.

The figure you twirl in your hand, you are watching for signs
of understanding, the figure already a wife rubbing against your palms,

already a ghost-wrapped voice who warns you to leave and to stay
and to burn your neighbor's birchbark supply and kill the three-legged dog

the meat sweet beneath its shag. What you're feeling is the bathos
of this house, the desperation of home melting the frameworks

meaning only to comfort your stay. The wife in your hand
sings nothing, will not face east as would the city's obedient dream.

You lap up water, you sing, you sit northernly. An air moves
the dark inside you as you watch with interest your object.

WITH DEAD BROTHER IN THE VENUS LANDSCAPE

How is it we stare at a word like *god* and feel the earth
shake but not you, dear *venus*. Around your stone I feel

the lakes of Europe ripple with forever drumbeats
and the footsteps out of this life. I have hung a reed

from a tree and wait for the sound of wind's disclosing
haunts to treat me kindly. As in kin. Twenty-five years in

and I am already sick, a cold broth on the table, one brother
gone. I am as in love with a man as I am with oil spills:

the world must flood and drain, men will pick at rock
until your gifts are found and named, but I don't

want to hear it. You, void of spells but of a kind
of vertigo, got *venus*, dun angel issuing nothing. An act

was done to my brother at the edge of a lake: blow air
through a reed long enough and he will go to you, believing.

RETOUCHING THE VENUS FIGURINE WITH FOCUS ON TORSO

I demanded a collection of accounts from you—
one could say *records* I say *dust* and I wanted *dust*

like an afterlife. The way you were so sweetly peeled
for instance, the face how it looked at you until

it looked to you. The brow gigantic and dying into you.
I could do it again you know. Shut my eyes and will

my starved and gaitless body through, the bristled wrists
of some gorgeous charlatan doomed to work her legs

to oblivion. I could make her catch in a mosquito's eye
I could make her almost nothing and she could stay fixed

as a stillborn the rest of infinity. If I am angry
it is because I miss no one the way I miss being monstrous

and small and mindless like you. I bless the sun
for its ability to snuff us, to busk the worms from our skin.

THE VENUS FIGURINE AS IT RELATES TO GNOSTICISM

I'm finding the alien has fled from you, you I'll call
daughter of the house now, your stone a dialogue in wandering

your beautiful woods through this world, and I'm sorry.
In part I have shucked you of coarse dwelling, yes I wanted

the walls to shake when I found you the way a door slams
when a man leaves for good. I am so happy for the second I

exist, when I hug this porcelain god for strength, when
your roundness makes me slight and ordinary.

When my bones are chains of midnight,
joints that snap and twine, my mother stands

over the stove, the sick village inside her. I want you my
the way is long and endless, my little cosmic terror. And out

the window the snow doesn't fall. I'm in love once and for all.

HOMECOMING WITH THE VENUS FIGURINE

Like a screen yanked open, my father suggested I come home
for an intervention. It wasn't food that I hated, but the stillness.

He who flung me into my body-stump, charged me the task
of water and air, manna from the bloody and starved hands

of so many defunct americas. Names are given to everything
that will ruin, even you one day. Let a man decree you *venus* and watch

what happens. I will return to his highway as soon as the sky
remains cold and I have removed myself completely from home.

The name of my strange dead brother doesn't hang from a tree
anymore. Let dust be the catastrophe of touch and let stone

be the crow in some ever-distant branch, the distal zone
you sit in now behind glass. The people who watch your idiot gaze

will all be gone a minute from now. If I crouched down
to pray, ever, it was only to feel my bruised knees.

INHERITING THE PALEOLITHIC ART ANTHOLOGY

To return to the home I found so many treasures there.
Piece of charred gutter, ash-soaked curtains, a cat jaw

jutted from dirt. A sunset pink as exposed fiberglass,
how still I became over those favors. A mattress blackened

where my girl-body once lay. When the fire took everything
I mean it was a confession, my house collapsed,

my animals dead. You were discarded, out of reach,
a footnote highlighted in my grandfather's great book.

Only then did you not exist. Only then did my girlhood
shape itself in a trailer.

If, years later, I took men through my bay window,
there was still a hill out back made of all of me smoked.

FIRST CONJECTURE OF THE SELF WITH FIGURINE

Tonight you are no one's treasure. There is a love
you've never craved carved into your limbs that I

want you to bury but don't. I swore I heard you out
in a clearing, the clearing I was made to feel

small and lost in, where I imagined you a cat coated
to a tree. There are no discoveries when an opening

is so vast no trees can grow to hide them in: People call this faith.
No discovery but for the cicadas that know to chirp

and collapse for the birds when the sky rolls back. When I eat
a meal I feel fat and marvelous as I did when the boys

kissed my neck against the house, too early in the night
to be known. I didn't shake out of fear. Sorry. They came

to my house crowded with sticks and I lost you out there. I believed
once that I drew my brother's ghost an impeccable likeness—

Like you, to tap one spot forever meant a piece of me stayed whole.
When I find home in my city, I will push your image back like a spleen.

WE WATCH AS IF WAITING FOR THE ARTIFACT TO OPEN HER EYES.

Since when have I ever told you what to do. Because
I am flummoxed, my imagination a luthier, my hands
a terrible suicide in which I break each beveled organ.
Understand I am useless. Understand the dead concrete
uprooted in a clearing is artless stone. I am pregnant
with another myth's god, you know. Your life will end
with the relief of dismounting a gaunt horse. Speak
of dignity, its sorry betrayal like strung goats.
That last kicked hoof is music, understand. The mission
is always to unbed these sordid mysteries, black museums
through which cornhusks privately exhume, mutant fur
I'll call my linsey-woolsey protects my soulless bilateria.
My strength disturbs your hearts. It must. From now on
you are only to speak to me bourbon-lipped. I will award you
an amulet: My body on a silver string, against your chest
heavy, unable to snap. It's simple to imagine me
there. Think of your cousin's body from its noose.
My burdens are entirely my own. How light they make us.

3

CONVERSATION WITH THE STONE WIFE

CONVERSATION WITH THE STONE WIFE

Define an opening. The way a snake learns. At the archaeology site,
being found was my greatest orgasm. The inarticulate erogenous map.

I dare you to bury me back to dirt and spinsterhood. I dare you.

The disgusting sun published my form, gave it culture, imagination. I loved
the nameless moment of rebirth, what you call war. Hands made only for my worship

is how I imagine cities. Sad reptilian scaffolds mouth our federal dreamscape.

So what if I was made in the snow of dying limbs. So what of my dead tribe.
I have a scientist now, *teams* of them. They trace me back, or bless their hearts,

they try. No wonder I'm bored. I have as much expression

in my eyes as when a debutante asks a man to draw her a bath. Instruct me
in the awful ritual of loneliness, so far I love its company, its gall of quiet

lovelessness. To be a man's specimen, I thought exile was the point of pleasure.

I am queen to the bathroom's yellow linoleum, the hair-scum in the drain
beautiful and mine. I have always been earth's least precious stone

but for the white-coats I'll grab at every sapling and thread to come again.

CONVERSATION WITH THE STONE WIFE

I could've been anyone when they found me, nook infant
ecstatic below your ice age. Look at me. I am gorgeous.

I dreamed there was such a scene as in a kitchen, a vague mother
bent over the sink devastated and safe. I keep waking up

in someone else's bed: awake inside a wolf's panting throat
is how I understand hunger. My loneliness is bikeable,

it is as though I have always worn a red cloak in the woods.
Teach me sorry. Teach me the trees. German darkness.

I worship the townhouses I so ritually leave, the waifish necks
of your citizens, and how there is one word for *snow* finally.

Lights stay on in too many locked houses. A squanderer
builds his kingdom into the ground. We forget to breathe

when we are instructed breath is continual. What I want touch to be
scatters flies in a neighboring basement, is as bountiful as tweed

in November. Mud husbands me to this terrible ordeal of burial.
But ruins bore me, I hate their gawked failure. Look to your own ugly sky.

CONVERSATION WITH THE STONE WIFE

Nothing interests me anymore. A garden is too enthusiastic
to be alive for its own sake. The highway, now that is something.
I want to be paved into colorless stone. Because you don't
believe me anymore and you've lodged with too many sisters,
am I correct in saying the engines of trucks sound arcane,
that you love the unbelievable smoke of winners? Define *desire*:
when have I ever made isolation difficult, it is my primary vocative
as when cars pedal their blood-speed down the interstate.
They bend as you, swerve around struck geese as you word
your desires. Define for me a body. I guess at its opposite: crows lift
heavily from power lines at the scattergun of a flabby man,
everywhere the smell of ersatz semen from dogwoods. Bereft.
These hours spin, are the aspirin dust of every horse gallop.
I've ceased my worries of being fathomed. I am stone. Sex.
No need for coddling, no need for linear paths of diction.
In the parade, I am a distant cousin's milktooth rattling
a mason jar. Someday the man with his gun will lift his legs
into a fabulous pair of corduroys. That sound will be a caw,
not the soundtrack of desiccated desert bones. But the highway:
crowded buses move the forsythia with definitive violence
in a way I know means I will never know touch. How cruel
to be so heavenly a body without body, the charge and wail
of skin and city and distance. Last winter the life of a battery
could poison the oceans forever—how could I tire of this?
Since then the Arctic seas have warmed. Disasters loom
with smug portending. I want to be opened, for someone's gaze
on my fissures. To be smelled for the ice age inside me.

CONVERSATION WITH THE STONE WIFE

When a dog learns to swim, what that does to language
is so important. Your voice quavers, the shape of an alphabet
inside your cheek dissolves like a town made of salt.
If you are interested, I am still wearing the gown this decade
required of me. Gold appliqué like a warship sinking
in circles. Oddly, the houses of a neighboring island have not caught fire.

CONVERSATION WITH THE STONE WIFE

You don't get to tell me my arms are useless. The kith
of scales should move you, the dedication
to impoverished architecture. Girlfriend, what you don't know is
I started gathering cotton grass in mock worship
of your romance with blackbirds. I started before you were born.
Dressed them in kohl, breathed my weathers into them.
You don't get to tell me the priority of wings. I know.
Cattails whip marshlands with the discipline
of a schoolmarm. I can tell you in the rain my labor is sexy.
My fat tits darken. I would lay down with anyone
who doesn't laud cloacae, irascible beaks.
That's ridiculous. All afternoon I grieved the great morning sky
you rode in on, prayed for its nothing change. See
how my English has improved. See how hot I look
descending the stairs, a choker of claws around my neck,
the talons dug into with arsenic. My old life bloats
like a collection of dictionaries abandoned beneath
the bed of some walk-up apartment. Hallelujah,
you've yet to get my magic. Already my veil appears silken,
my spiderleg lashes. Leave me my materials, my histrionics.

CONVERSATION WITH THE STONE WIFE

I am extremely interesting. Have lived in my colonial house
like a boasting pilgrim many years. Each night I fork liver
into my disciplined body and pull curlers out of my hair

to make love to the bunched-up duvet. I wrote you
about my blondest moment: my Bulgarian tongue twisted
with my Swahili tongue, the blond voice spiraling out

in a fit of healthy aggression. Blond melodies. Blond cramps.
Blond mules I ride through my blond village. I wrote you
to suffer the nice girl, snort her frankincense down

with our normal animal cruelties. Yesterday I played my navel
like a bent harp until the sky stood up to that drab darkness
I keep telling you about: airplanes look like antique stars I hate.

Give me something I can use.
I admire any man who lets the epochs bury him, a spoon

rusting his mouth shut so beautiful. Yes I'm another oversexed girl,
my body hurts me. A building on fire gives me cat eyes.
I move there too. Touch my golden hips and I'll never eat again.

CONVERSATION WITH THE STONE WIFE

Like you, my creator was flawed. But see
                    I am perfect. See.
I didn't ask my body to be called up, those darling
                    perverts
made me like they couldn't make a clit sing.
                    You taught me pain
I'm not finished. It tasted of fennel, my tongue
                    a stranger in diplomacy.
I wanted temptation, to fixate on the flanks
                    of doomed steers.
How could pleasure matter on the blade
                    of the godknife.
I am but one moment of oblivion and fact.
                    Your towers
are as dull a fiction as my headdress.
                    How would
anyone buy into that gesture. Fool's city.
                    Esurient shoppers.
All the plates scrape clean, that hunger
                    should disgust you more.
I'm trapped in the gaze of an open mouth.
                    My form is
an open mouth, it is closing in time with
                    the shockless guts
which make massive your cities. My god am I
                    at my most beautiful.

CONVERSATION WITH THE STONE WIFE

Talk the dog out of me. The fearless brute the great text lauds.
You think it mattered that my stone darkened in the rain.

My promises are the same jar you'd store marmalade in before January's
shut doors. The house is dead. What's of import

is the scarf on the aborigine neck–
whether cool or damp I know its cloth doesn't warm just any girl.

I am not the cow I was, not the grass on the field, not the ball the men
applaud in sweaty worship.

Look how my hands form at the mention
of forever. My sweetly diminished chin.

The decades dress themselves
in a wardrobe of rat spit and lysol. Divine in every country.

Look how the decades suture panic to every hissing swan.
There's so much religion in the tall grass along the highway edge,

I'll wear the skull of every smashed raccoon until I feel as immortal
as I am. I am so immortal. In all these years I said nothing profound.

4

[letter excavated from the willendorf tomb]

Whoever said *dry* is the word for a life of solitude didn't account for my rhetoric, my depth of absolute distance. You display me as you please: blue dress, white dress, pink dress, yellow dress. My face is always the same spent splendor as the girls who self-portrait the internet over. You know the ones, N. *Mad angels.* I feel stuffed to the brim with alibis and strappy dresses. The world doesn't want me but the world has awful taste. You spoil me with your excellent taste, N. You protect me from the dirt that seeks to claim me again, and I just don't know why since in a wink you'll be dead and I'll have flexed not even a lash to interfere as you darken with vinegar and stop. Alibi: a man had to unbury me more than once to claim me timeless but my eyes were sealed shut against the dirt and worms and metals, I was a sexy insect god the world couldn't recognize for its gross preoccupation with man. Alibi: man hands himself his letters of will when I am a film of closeups played backwards. I've no means to see my importance. Why should I apologize if all this time I have wanted to birth the most perfect child in the most perfect dress. Jesus, N. These mad men a wind of psychic distance.

NOTE TORN FROM THE WIFE-BOOK AFTER THE STORM

I keep thinking about the sorceress. She ages
in the rainshadow like an orphaned hat
in a far-flung city. I rode my first donkey yesterday
while Mahler composed silver gods
inside storm funnels. I suppose I miss our children.
A tall man let me eat chia from his hands,
me in a dress so pink I fell drunk against Corinthian
columns. Irresistibly portraiture. I starve
my skin like my loose hair, her numinous static.
Say what you just said to the crowd to me.
I've slurped down harder cocktails than that. See
I'm interested in the sorceress: the witch-flowers
inside every cabinet bloom cumin and tarragon, I've snapped
every plastic fork left steeping blank
in the drawers. The magic of shed light is we get to
say *shed light*, but that isn't what makes me
astonishing. While organ meats boil into gravy,
I've dreamt up a new Aphrodite: she is in a sea
too shallow to reach any shore of earth—stranded
she fucks herself, learns every feasible version
of *accident*, again fucks herself until the waters warm to her body
and rise. That's why I feel so at home here.
I taped the refrigerator doors shut in anticipation
of the surge. Left your chicken roasting in the oven.
I dream that fish swim because they were promised sharper teeth
one day. When a great storm takes our poorest homes
I'll fling open these doors like tremendous wind to see
my grayed sorceress, stoned and ambling
to her straw bed, condensed milk cans strewn at her feet.
We have names for such women: yesterday's newspaper
floating in a pool, a single missing fork, the Finnish
word for *green*. I swear I'm the truest Anne of all.

NORTHEAST OF ARUBA

I will consider your blunder a golden egg
if only you'd reach into the darkness
after my mother. She is with the last shade
of lipstick between a fir and an aged goat.
She is forgetting her gray hair in praise
of forgetting. The field is a disorder of wheat,
it means I am helpless. I folded her dresses
into a chest long ago, smoothed and crossed
the sleeves before locking it completely.
The chest was a shipload of a great parrot's eggs
sorry to say. I am sure they were buried
in a soft bed of dirt. I dreamed it was Aruban sand
I brushed off the lid, each dress was a body
she slept in. Men rose to visit her from their posts:
before they laid tracks I stopped them
at the trees, slipped bundles of twine behind
their ears. The sound of a fox paw on grass
means I'll keep searching the leaves for her rings.
The agony of loss is its refusal
to be a vocabulary. I worry astonishment
is an anecdote for decay: she walked to the sea
with a busted guitar slung over her back.
Dresses all over a shore look like shot angels.

I WANT A LOVE

At a certain altitude it was the man over me over the couch
A paperback flopped open to an insignificant page as the basement leaked

Water a study of scales study of want study of my hair on his chest
His chest breathing his password of night the moon a lacquered nail its

Insouciance trickling white sound in my brain the village a limp hand
Mindlessly open as in sleep as in death he is sleeping I am sleeping

Overpeopled but I want a love as simple as a peacock feather brushing me
A peacock feather boasting eyes and black cry against this tin crack of earth

The planet buckling its new gait a bomb renting a crowded bus but
I called this a city a place to store my men and wives a place for talking

Fucking under a handsome sun the men string fish from the harbor bury
Chicken feet in the sand all this oil embossed in our eyes dredging us

Billions of legs wrapped around billions of legs I want a love to remove me
From all countries from Sangiovese cocoa cow be reversible the village

Stacked over me patting my bare spine I want a love to tell me I am responsible
Let me stop us I want a love to sleep with my women sneak abortions

Record my seven billion promises to dirt and steaming plates instead this man
In the village he turns me on my side he sings my singular love gets swallowed

CONSIDER A LANDSCAPE

Consider a landscape. Now take it away. Who can speak of this world
and call its moldering hills worth depiction. Remember to love its trash
because like it you didn't ask to be made. Because there is a wind here

that hurts like a yellow color, here a city, here a stranger who, having
traveled a century's length, asks to lie down in your lap. I love what

your lips do when you refuse this man the dignity, that neutral twitch.

We share a poverty, its bread-type and halal. I will forgive the plastic
filling my stomach with each prewrapped sandwich I will forgive

the wisteria's track with a cigarette burn. I made a city of wax paper,
forgive the stray lettuce, forgive the mayonnaise, forgive these yarn
citizens in their yarn walk-ups. Who invited this man? The stranger he

wants to teach me truth, to write a book as small as my waist, but this
fool, I invented truth too. Come now the ocean is filling with seagulls

and I must be allowed to speak of my feminism while also telling
M how fat I'm getting in this size 2 dress. The stranger wants me
to say *river* and *pelt* and *opera gloves*. Well, all night a mud river

flowed out of me, I pulled up my opera gloves, the night a barrier,
a deliberate pelt, my mother dies every night here, then my father.

My grandmother a deader moon, the chemical light of dead stone

I drink hard inside. My body collapses without me, the bourbon of

smoked angels digitizing my bored blood. And yes I am too often
not hurting god, I'm so in love I've given it skin. There are conditions

to this existence I didn't ask to be made into. To be in love means death stones over, I'll never be made this vulgar and spent again.

IMPRECATION

Balm of fallen girls, balm of dog bladder
loose from its body. I kept you like
a smuggled feather, the journey
vast and untelling. I had a wife, thrown
broken crystal at my feet. Balm of homely
deer-gods, cold smoke of the tribe
that made you, that sculpted you stone
over beveled stone. I had a mother
whom I loved for your likeness—
buxom, tearing at the seams.
Like you she watched my declension
not unkindly. Like you she found
edges and stayed just there. Balm then
of fixed skin. The spine able to love
able to snap like safety and undo
all signs of breath, my dumb privileges.
I made a list of pets sacrificed
over the course of a thousand years,
none told in your name. I had a wife
made of stitches, worms curled
in the seams, and you were a footnote
to *artifact*, my broken legs and arms.
Balm of coconut for the stretch marks
on my buried dogs. I had a city of limestone,
your body collecting as we drank
rainwater, the nerves in our throats.
I had a spell for all comers
they made flint replicas of you
they gave you eyes and you watched them
marvel you watched them drown
and gouge and smother each other.

I had a city of women, we practiced
self-immolation we practiced kissing
the men who would finish us.
I had a city made I had a city.

EPITHALAMIUM

Be at the lake at the snow at the tree. The garbage bags cramp
all around us, hard cakes, dead rats, milk water, you mean

the world to a minute, V. A cigarette disgusts the dirt, your waistline
a tumored swan guarding the empty lake. Enough, I don't much

like you, oolitic wife, be at the lake at the snow at the tree, take
your familiar path to that spot in my liver my uncle withered in.

Veil opens to a thirst for red, the dark space in my wrist where
no riverman sent for his letters. I mean a door is just a question

hardened to a threat: At the lake at the snow at the tree
a bridegroom texts a phone since disconnected, your headdress

the hands of a comet field tonight. In the consummate bed you
strip your onion skins, you crown yourself queen, you drip

your urtext into my sleeping ear, you crown me unpublished,
you mistake me for fragments. Never could love be more like

a busted television facedown on a bed, I betrothed and becoming
the come mythologized inside me. You poor scalloped wrench

you were made to be a tool, you were made to be at the lake
at the snow at the tree, your history a birch's dead braille. I only

love you when you fit in my palm, when the trash takes itself
to a lake to poison the lake. What good is a lake if a boy doesn't

drown swimming to a girl on the other side. You taste my tang.
You hold the frozen swan to my mouth. I watch the black trees.

[letter excavated from the willendorf tomb]

N, madness took the comb from my hair, removed the mantle surrounding my nights, and exposed me for the brilliant bitch I am. I admire your patience, the way you twirl your hair fantastic to have me and have me again. I admit I'm sore and spoiled of all this coddling. No wonder I keep wandering the halls clubbing my ears, there is a music coming from one of these doors and I am too locked inside my stone carapace to stop any of this from flooding. *N*, we've been working together for years and aren't you bored of the clumsy balance between language and identity and aren't you even the smallest bit disappointed with your lack of honest engagement in me as a subject, how I don't think it matters one bit to you whether or not I last forever or burn to kohl ruins in my museum cage tomorrow. I don't blame you, *N*. You write poems. You work in an office forty hours a week and come home nightly with a vague despair nestled against your spine when what you want is to be shattered and tearing the skin of your face until a new governance seals over your bones and someone publishes your book. I am so fond of you I would publish your dry skin cells, *N*, I think it will last the test of time so long as I keep it close. Isn't it strange, I know, what we do with the men of this world to be known.

OLD WIVES' TALE

You hear me you are to meet me by the horse lake the one
sick with horse parts where children swim, water gushing

from their mouths. I can't stand any of it. I am forever barefoot
for the worms to wriggle my soft female skin. To be butter,

to be the wolf in heat: now a cloud forms over the lake to welcome
nothing, a family in blind procession. Means someone I love will die.

Means I will walk from a distance toward a man with a shovel.
Know that I have cracked the skin of love to discuss what

patterns of body fit that liminal space where I fever.
There is a certainty in the wings of a bat. In the house I can think

of nothing but home's symbol. I was a boy before a bowl of milk,
I was a boy before they grew rhizome in the garden, before

they pulled every bit of flesh from the dirt. I made all the rings
swing in the house. Today I dressed all the changelings in tweed

and destroyed all evidence of their origins. They will love me
goddamn it they will love me. You are to meet me with a dead owl

in your messenger bag. You are to quash black snails on every porch.
Gravedigger, every morning I curse my days. I look so good doing it.

EPITHALAMIUM

You do look beautiful distending the stairs but wait there wait,
I'm removing a splinter from my toenail, I wedged the flint in
I needled it out. It's like how you enter a room on all fours unable
to walk without crinoline soughing down a hallway. This house
is endless, the guest list unbearable. I can't walk three feet
without kicking a can. After the ceremony I will fill
the bathtub with flat beer to soak you until
I can drive a comb through your stone hair. Believe me
when I say I'm tired of your looks, your thoughts, your voice,
your all-cosmic power, it makes my dick soft. What happens
between two people is not impossible, I'm just saying I've lain down
in the center of worse storms and still my own animal has a taste
for gutters. Your nude face bores me. Try a blush. Try two.

GALAXY MEAT

It matters how you speak of failure. The term lover.
            I have never used this term outside poetry.

Why *lover*, monsieur croque, when what I mean is
dah-na-na-na-na-na-na, dah-na-na-na-na-na-na,
dirtbag. I guess it lacks the pert trochee. The exact volte-face.

I speak of failure the way one might salt meat, the water
of the animal comes up through the muscles to praise
your hunger with a meatsong. I fork my failures until tender.

Certain unreal terms: watermeat, failprotein, tearcartilage.
            I have more feelings of being meat than being a lover.

There was a girl about your age who queened herself
in front of her personal mirror. Pushed back the skins
to get a closer look, queenly inspections a sign of choice propriety.

Desperate for narrative she consulted her gargoyle nook,
the pink cleanse underneath where no one dared finger.
She could wake up. She could be the kind of girl who woke up.

I placed this anecdote here like a toytruck on a carpet
            to evoke something about place and the dumb decades of girlhood.

But I want to live inside the coils of a menstrual rug, and for salt
to sing me out of my troubled blood. Lately I've dreamed
of nothing but my girlfriend in a pink tulle dress collapsing
in the road. I wake up and pink lace crowds my eyes in hot yoga.

The naked women in this dressing room are my lovers,
the yoga bodies and the yoga bodies and the yoga bodies,

I place them on the back of an ampersand I'll never use,
they ride away like galloping horses.   *&&&&&&&*

These naked women virgin-oil themselves into horizons.
Grateful for the opportunity. I am the kind of sunset
that can store the world's goods without a speck of responsibility.

Speak of failure, says the girl to her figurines. The term
failure of imagination is a *failure of imagination*
so don't throw that shade on my legion of rich oiled twats
when the problem is clearly we're beautiful shitty idiots.

I wrote a poem about a horse named Galaxy once (ugh)
and all the boys gave me treats they said, wow lady wow
this is such a pretty, pretty poem

I HAD GRAND NOTIONS OF THE PASTURE

Inside the eyes of a Christian, my doom
wears a negligee. In my stretched tunic
I pinch my cheeks to give them blush.
I am the color of a pursued wife. Feed me.
A cupful of spinach. Imagine my shock
a purple cauliflower when you pin me
with your beautiful knee down. Shiitake
breath fervent on my neck, I had notions
that crow's feet rose from the ground
like a botched idea. Allow me to follow
through: a truck is shattering my illusions
of grandeur, but I love this idea of rendering
the skin of an unborn face over my worries.
I drove a tractor on empty over the lavender,
the catastrophes clean and florid on my tongue.
You could sketch the complexity of my thoughts
out with cornstarch. That I'm simple is valid.
At my most perfect, rust crumbles apart
on the opening hinge of an antique car door.
Nothing demonstrates change better than
a drowning fly in oil. I fell in love
with a pastry chef for the mechanical care
in her eggwashing. And you expect to teach me
sorry. I swell with child, petroleum shakes the leaves.

INVENTING THE ETYMOLOGY OF MY NEWEST COUNTRY

How did it work: I carried a machine
on my back from one field

to a tundra, made a tomb in my name,
the objects I claimed.

Assembled the ashes like they were a thing
in need of assembly.

One raises a flag this way. I pledged
once like pulling a wasp's

sting from my chest, its abdomen
wriggling my beautiful statehood.

I carried a machine on my back
from a tundra to a new northwest.

Wanted to speak with my *I* voice. Forgot.
I renamed my collective

to forget again, to disgrace and perturb
an east of here. How I licked each

flower to determine its origins with fruit,
or the skin of a woman's

pain. The soil was a way to speak to
the tenderly flensed beasts,

the sawgrass the silence in a boy's slapped cheek.
Nothing made me whole

or decent or sad as the thought that within
a swan's neck was more liquid.

How I worshipped loneliness if loneliness
could mean once *I was the cold spit*

you had to swallow in a hospital cot.
Took the train to a village:

I wanted to be skin in its small world
and for that moment

to redefine conquest. With my semaphore
I raised a flag

that could wipe the god from any man's face.
I carried my machine still

to a bog. Dumped it there the way a bullet
enters say an elephant's heart.

When the elephant's heart won't quit
and we fail again at mercy

this means my country, the sinking
of its metal a new form of prayer.

EPITHALAMIUM

You are too late to the scene:
how sad that we come from branches,
your dress snagged by branches.

I am already waking up
in a quarry, the everywhere nests

of your busy work, the April wind
a continuum of our falling bed.
Too often the poem tells us to find a lake.

I left a bridegroom bleeding
in a warehouse to live in this gone day,

I don't know a thing about crawling
on my knees, just the liquor of ritual,
just the way your face means bruised stone

in the warmest light. The screaming match
of a city and a city gives your eyes color.

Your hips roan-thick with mysterious age.
Too often we greet change with soft dignity
the way a forest does the arrival of men.

In this sky a plastic fog lacks the right poison
and I will certainly never die. If we dance,

I wanted to dance. Cocktails warm to gel
all around us, my throat fills with sequins
in the middle of this terrible field.

SWAN MEAT

Why do you look so angry all the time.
Smile. I have placed your flesh delicately in tin,
sealed it shut, designed a periwinkle label.
There is nothing to worry about. No one
worries over the image of a beautiful swan.
My spear cracked your breastbone with a swiftness
so exact I ran home to my wife to cry
in her lap over life's constant perfections.
Her lap smalled with my tears of gratitude
and suddenly every limb smalled too on her.
What miracles! You can split birch with an ax
all day long but the women you want always stay
the same size? What are you doing, neon goose,
with your wild hair and your split tits and this hip
to waste ratio. Don't look a man in the eye
if you don't entertain the fantasy of a hack
hack hack of his [my] blade on your neck.
I smell your bottoms, your flat feet orangeing
my cock into new and gradual definitions
of *system*. Men choose what animals bleed,
what animals purr. Because of me you'll
never be the acid-spitting wife of nothing.
I want to digest your proteins but won't:
you're better in the package, better steeped in juice,
plum-sick and plucked until yonic,
in the connubial sweat of death and its promise.
Believe it that no one will taste the difference
in the way you chose to spread those wings.
Remember to smile for the fork and you'll be
swallowed down with gold, gold soda.

[letter excavated from the willendorf tomb]

And did it occur to you in all these years that I could speak for myself. You're a good girl, *N*, you stick to your books. Let us say I've moved on, I've rented the city for one year's time and will not stop fucking these scared little boys. There is a fog over the towers, they hover and putrefy in Ozymandian disgrace. Pastries clog the gutters and I've never had such a fat ass fat breasts fat hands, this fat my beautiful beautiful. I've gone dizzy with drink, *The Philadelphia Story* won't stop playing and I won't ever get over the bored portrait of godhood in Katharine Hepburn's waistline. There will never be enough milkshakes so far as I'm concerned. *N*, I know how worried this makes you. I've seen your food diary, your "kale salad no dressing." Look on my waist ye sham citizens. There's a smell to me, it's almost human. My god, *N*, these men do throw a good party if you're not paying attention to the noise so heteronorm. I would die were I not so perfectly timeless. Lord knows you've been keeping track. Relax and have a drink. I'm a good wife now let me speak.

5

THE DEATH & LIFE OF THE VENUS CITY

1. ON THE CONFRONTATION WITH MEN & HISTORY

The Venus of Willendorf limped from a dirt ocean
in 1908 into the hands of one Dr. Josef Szombathy.
She was not meant to worship a god not meant to god
in any woods any city any open field. Like a good
woman-object she would be used as a channel. The men
to fill her fat with seed, avocado, desire, reed music.

Either she was not a god or not a good god.

Such holy qualifiers never occur to draftsmen.
Nothing but a vision filled in dark with rock.
Nothing but the mimesis of riches. A handsome particular
to fill with anthropological myth, another chance
for men to theorize *those people*.

I would like to decline the invitation here to call her
a goddess, a fertility goddess no less. Jean Markale
wrote about her as the "Universal Great Mother" but
I thought a woman's age hides in her hands. I'm tired today,
wish only our beautiful women dead and scattered
beneath the earth. When a woman is magnificent
don't you dare with the drowsy moniker *goddess*.
Szombathy knew no better, and why should he,
he's king of every ancient civilization under his site.
Archaeologists who penetrate the hidden layers of creation
with their tools, who pick out bombed-out Eden,
who name these objects to line their kingdoms.

Blegh.

So Western to suck on the world until it's sticky
with gospel and dirge. Call the shapely stones unearthed
Venus, let them fly down all witchy and worn

to serve as the imbeciles' lorddess. See what I care.
I'm not even born yet. I will grow into an overeducated
administrative assistant I will grow into a small thing
on a crowded train who stares at a sick old woman and thinks:
At what age does a woman's body become the insult of a woman's body.
I will be nobody's wife, just a special someone's car alarm.

I will end up calling the Venus of Willendorf
my queen and we will end up
fucking under the hood of her legendary cunt
until my skin disappears and she stays immortal.
It is easy to be guilty of the things you so righteously
profess. She was found in 1908, a leap year,
the same year oil was found in the Middle East.
There is no document of civilization
that isn't also its ruins. When you ask for nature,
you end up with another incompetent god.

2. HOW HUNGER, HOW HORSE

At first the Venus of Willendorf ate a whole epoch of dick.
She was hungry and lonely, buried deep in the earth so obscure
for most of her life she didn't even exist.
When finally Szombathy touched her, nerves tore her awake
it was like biting into a high voltage battery. He found her
dry-humping shale, the loess perfuming her form.
An unenlightened mind might call this encounter
the purest form of love, the kind of love one only finds
between man and his newest possession. I knew better
in 1708 I knew better then in 1908 in 2008 in 2108
that when a man finds something this earthshattering
this monumental it is not love he finds but certainty.
To name, to be language, to be an erect footnote
in this small glimpse of existence. I go to work

and do not resist gazing at my own reflection
in the passing building glass. I worry my hips'
steady expansion, the genealogical curse of our women.
Don't worry about the heat of passing trucks, that deathwish wind.
I'm in my windowless office and would slaughter
a lamb for just an extra inch of space, that's joy alright.
The Venus of Willendorf must have lost her taste
for cock, must have lost herself the way women

lose themselves in the midst of a moor.
A woman must always lose herself in the *midst*. The mist.

The whatever myth. Of a colorblind sky and the beautiful iceland
where hands conceived her. Hands are a touch
of information over the tits, the headdress, the neglected
sight of her fat flat ass. I know about being carved,
it's a starvation ritual, it's the skin pulling tight around bones,
it's the stony pain when sitting on the subway. Carved

as the hair falls out, carved as the cuticles yellow and wax.
Carved when the flesh dares us be bovine—and we don't.
Her beauty like an oilcloth trashed on a rainy day.
I'll starve it out to wear it like the cloth of a flag,
an allegiance founded in the vinegar bruise of an arm.

I think of Muybridge's horse. And horse. And horse. And horse. And horse.
That's the sun in this city setting and setting and setting.

3. THAT SPECIAL SOMEONE

That's when the people set out to make her,
when the world appeared to happen every day.
In truth there was no mystery. There were animals,
blades were made, and then there were pelts
and meat against the deathwinds. Survival
became a specific kind of boredom, a boredom
in which you taste blood in your mouth, nails
in your back, sex at the end of your thighs,
the body in starvation mode. The kind of boredom
millennia later paleontologists would call *harsh*

living conditions. The Venus of Willendorf
plopped out of the cranium with unrivaled ceremony.
All those cold limbs death would cure,
they conceived of a creation, we collected it,
we gave it neurological explanation to better
map the early hominid brain. The Venus of Willendorf
chomped on every frozen nub, she looked into
their dying sockets like an oil-drum and dear Europe
grew as grass over their skulls. Poor them.

Journalists approach the Venus of Willendorf
with questions every day while she files her nails
and thinks the perfect blankness of an equator line.
They follow her up the stairs. They ask "But Mrs.—
Miss—Willendorf, when you were alone all those years
was there a special someone's hands rotting
violently to pebbles near you that gave you strength?"
"Who is your ideal sexual partner?"
"Who are you wearing tonight, Miss Willendorf?" And when
she turns around she sucks long and hard on their mics
and the orgasm they share is tremendous.
We simply don't know how to escape empire do we.

4. PEAK SHIFT EFFECT

The Venus of Willendorf and I eat a whole cake
in the park on my lunch break. I ask her about our kingdom
regularly and she belches, she breaks a can
on her faceless head, she demands half n' half.
I'm sorry I can only offer her queenship, she wilds
for nothing but calories and sex: the food is decent this year,
there's so much more decadent trash. I throw up buttercream
in a nearby dumpster I just can't keep up with her appetite.

At the bakery, I explain the neurological term *peak shift effect*
to the cashier, she gives me my change, she thanks me
for choosing their catering service. I was six
when a man first found me, eleven when I first found
the Venus in Grandpa Leo's anthology, already a plump
and golden girl. I wrote her fan mail in careful words:

HOW MANY TOUCHED YOU BEFORE YOU TOUCHED BACK?

She didn't respond, she just showed up one day years later
with a whole crate of plastic-wrapped pastries.
The lengthy ingredient list said EAT UP! and we did.
The theory of *peak shift* goes that when man
is deprived of those Western, god-given rights like
potatoes and burgers and shelter, he expresses
this deprivation by exaggerating what he lacks.
So, hairless clawless fangless men make war their legacy.
So, a wary people struggling through an ice age *may*
depict their women with fat tits fat hips a stupendously warm slit.

I spend my whole life sexualized and pinned
only to feed and feed and feed my new stone wife
who asks for nothing but absolute indulgence.
At night I line our bed with styrofoam, straws,

marmalade jars. I remind her that we still need to talk
about empire and federal laws and whether or not
our citizens will respond to our wars
with a few heated letters. But delivery is almost here.
Yes, the delivery is almost here.

5. DR. SZOMBATHY RECEIVES OUR LETTER

Without fail, it's me, V, and Szombathy engaged in a threesome.
It is so easy to maneuver a rock in heat but the doctor
believes his dick the real miracle here. Sometimes
I remember that I am someone's daughter. It's raining again.
Mid-thrust is the only time *V* speaks, this time she says
The death and life of great American cities is about
negotiating influences and the impressions of citizens.

This session will involve a great deal of capitalism.

I try to remember the last time I said the word tribe
without irony, without taking the length of my history
inside me. *A city is not a work of art it does not show*

our humanity nor can it represent its own artifact,
she goes on and on this way. Szombathy
on my shoulders waits to banish us and all I want
is to disappear with *V* under a bridge to gaze from below
at the wonders of our city. Strangers enter me
and I respond with silence, but *V* she's an anti-city

no man can enter her. She was expressed as a vessel
without a vessel, hands combed over her breasts
she was designed to be taken in a pocket elsewhere,
isn't that how I will become a wife isn't that why
I call her stone wife, why I take her with me into
the harbor, under the ground and into the tunnels,

why I feed her my meals and stand over her girdle-less
and foul. *The self-destruction of a city*, *V* says in the midst
of an orgasm. *The relentless competition of a space*
until its primary economic function becomes
the loss of its function. When the good doctor leaves

I read my queen from the couch to the bed.
There is an absence in the room like a freezer door
left open all night, the cold touching even
the moon's dead holes. Starvation cools my feet
she calls me corpse feet, I fetch her some cheese.
V has a hard time accepting Szombathy as anything
but a god. I'm sorry so many times midworship.

6. IN THE MOOD FOR LOVE

We were out of Netflix and the sun was shining. We both cried
all the way through *In the Mood for Love* and now it was time
to enter that great city fit for the laziest gods. We were happy.

Things between us were becoming less funny. Szombathy
sent us 500 loose birthday candles the day we announced
our engagement, and what we could only determine to be
the hoof of an elk fawn. At the botanical gardens, I spied
a cluster of snapdragons and thought of my mother
letting her car run in the garage during the great black out
of two thousand three. *V* needed ice cream

and that's when I wept for the first time over this image.
She didn't need this, she needed cream and fudge
in a waffle cone. Too many man-made lakes
make up gardens, too many flowers and birds
attempt a kind of sick nature. Some people

recognized *V*, strange when they don't really,
but they just kept their eyes forward and fixed
like good passers-by. At the truck, I asked for
a waffle cone for my beautiful fiancée and the crook
leaned forward on his elbows to ask if that'd be all
this Wednesday morning.

At a certain point, my hair fell out in chunks.
Never had I experienced love beyond one little
heartbreak, some hairline fracture
I would add it to the great ledger of obscurity and pain.

So what if people die, I collect bowls now
to collect the dust. *V* was normalizing
to this city's earthling ways but still

couldn’t go to a garden without pissing
under a rose bush. We would marry next summer.

Blackbirds started dropping dead from the sky.

7. (THE MORNING OILS STAIN BEHIND MY NAILS)

I'm in love, I said Yes maître d', put our names down
we'll sit at the bar while we wait. We're the kind of couple
content to say nothing most of our meal, *V* only ever
muttering Jane Jacobs and the lost journals of Doctor
Szombathy incoherently. I'm beginning to believe
the doctor isn't real, that this is a Tyler Durden situation
and the world will rupture while *V* chants urban planning

and its failures. It's nice though, the orchestra of silverware
and espresso steamers and all that red lipstick giddy
over mimosas. My hands look aged, the sick skin

of a mule, and I'm beginning to appreciate *V*'s luxuries
in being handless, barely able to stand upright without
a cute little prop. (I have opened so many cans.) (Touched
myself too much too sad.) (Held my hair back to throw up
a recent meal I will never be skinny enough.) I wrote *V*
more than one piece of fan mail before she arrived for good.

WHEN WOMEN SLEEP DO THEY SLIP UNDERGROUND WITH YOU?

WHAT STOPS BROTHERS FROM STOPPING HUNGRY MEN?

ATTACHED, YOU'LL FIND MY RÉSUMÉ AND PHOTO. I LOOK FORWARD
TO HEARING FROM YOU.

The camcorder got us jumping on a bed, we had on
matching capotes, I was of age, we were in our midsts
and the country was lost in our web of blissful trash.
I was ready to have her baby, Szombathy would make
the necessary arrangements so we could have our favorite
scents blend together: mine, sage and lavender, hers,

caramel and hamburgers. I wanted to decorate the honeymoon suite based on Dickinson's repeated use of the word *abstemious*:

MAKE AN ABSTEMIOUS ECSTASY
NOT SO GOOD AS JOY

V argued by way of silent ravenous appetite,
in protest vomited a long time along the corridor walls.

8. WEDDING REGISTRY

Tri-tip sandwich with onion rings and chocolate hazelnut milkshake.

Macaroni and cheese and lobster and truffle and bourbon and the hands
will they ever leave me and sage butter.

Triple mocha, the leaves budding on the trees, five almond biscotti dunked murderously.

Brussels sprouts, duck confit, parmesan fries, Charles Olson's *The Maximus Poems,*
love nothing but the moment teeth scrape grease from the bone, I stay inside it.

Lion curry, beast of burden nan, dragon retreating into the desert with
my infancy, snow falling out the window in Brooklyn, my happiness a cracked lens
but effective, always effective as the naked sun blares cold on bare limbs.

Triple mushroom spring roll, banana split, will the sun ever come back and warm
my legs, steak-frites, broken martinis, ruinous syrup is mint.

9. WHAT DOOM?

The biographer will be here soon, to explain why I'm so dressed up.
Why these jittery, pre-wedding feelings. It would be impossible
to explain everything: the earth split open and revealed an entire id
in early human civilization, desire pivotal in all creation myths
including this one, the one we type placards in museums about,

when *V* broke out of her jail to find me, Amnesty International
used *V* in their campaign to promote their new commitment
to Paleo Rights, or as the various media called it "The Great Mother Project."
It all gets quite entangled in chronology and miracles.

V is finishing up her veal filet in the other room. The city is massive
and she is always hungry for something inside it. I'm wearing
the shorts I wore every day the summer of 1995 but they are full
of holes now and just a small bit more sexual.

The sun is just about ready to hurt us and I bless it for its abilities

to stare into every invention with easy rapture, I'm afraid
for its heats, as afraid of this nature as I am of the sight of a god
sharpening its killing knives in the kitchen sink.

V's hunger is as peculiar as a parrot in a branch, I can't
keep up with the trays they stick to the carpet facedown.
I told the biographer she would only speak to him
if he brought her rice pudding and to orgasm.
He asked how she liked tiramisu. I told him the world was ending,
but would end with everyone tasting something sweet on their tongues.

He won't be asking any more questions of me. Sweet onion perfumes
every room of this house, I swear the doom is sweet.

6

CHIAROSCURO

The worry is always whether my indulgence like a regular subject-predicate is universal.

The worry is whether the scope of my writing now rests too firmly on autobiography and the sexual violence of autobiography.

Does the writing inure itself to the act, does it inflict too much falsity around the feelings, and what exactly even is a trigger.

I will not indulge I will not indulge I will not indulge.

My honeymoon with the Venus of Willendorf ended in the same bucolic lyric in which it began.

The field felt different then. Warmed and flattened by a body. The shade and storm of having been present is how we annihilate the sequence leading to now. I'm not sure if this body is mine.

Which is to say I am tired of poets describing nature in the correlative sense.

A stranger handed me a narrative of my life, and another made of stone.

I whittled a symbol in the shape of my body and handed it back.

Wrong. Imprecise. I am more fragile than the narcissist who lives in a glass dustbowl with her selfies. Sparrow-lipped alone with her followers mortally following.

This morning the city smelled of a brush-fire seventy miles away and I felt a pang of uncertainty followed by grief and it is chiefly for this reason that I cannot clearly communicate with animals or men.

Why is it only now that we smell that distant burning.

When I say *stone* do I mean a rock in a prettier pretense. Will the stone kill less against the temple. If I say the word that was done to me then I will become the act that was done to me.

I want love in the eating season, the white sun to whittle my body from prosecco flutes into the negation of bodily needs.

Progression broke down into figurines long ago. I cheated the fat out of progress to snuff out progress and look at my city, just look at it.

At night I fall asleep with my teenager scene still in my head, and its brutality coaxes me away, apart, into a capsule of safety.

Grandma Willendorf showers with me under her legs the next morning. I taste her residue, tarry nectar of her hovering belly.

I wanted to write this empty, disavowed of the tweets of universal pangs.

Disavowed again of my fumbling history. Forget forget forgetting.

Now as always it is difficult for us to see smoke without the interpretation of fire following after.

I read one detail of drone warfare in which its victims curse the clear sky, the blue coming from space down as a killing target, the drone's narcissism needing the closeness of its shadow. Its bodily needs.

I've reviewed the terms of this contract and removed all maudlin clauses, all the melodramas of my finite skins. Now only the rock queens remain. The word *no*. No.

A helicopter razes the weather, fogged and becalm of smoke. My city snuffed in a bright modern weather, snuffed in a weather with no trigger in sight.

Notes

Some ideas and phrases in *The Death & Life of the Venus City* borrow from Jane Jacobs's *The Death and Life of Great American Cities.*

Some ideas and italicized phrases in the Venus Figurine poems borrow from Hans Jonas's *The Gnostic Religion*.

Jean Markale's *The Great Goddess* was instructive in thinking about and constructing many of the "Venus" of Willendorf poems.

Some of the "Conversation with the Stone Wife" poems borrow phrasing and the language of smug privilege from Katharine Hepburn in *The Philadelphia Story*. If any voice should be in your head for those, it's hers.

ACKNOWLEDGMENTS

Some of the poems in *Swan Feast* have appeared in journals in various iterations. Thank you to the editors of the following journals for featuring these poems: *Adirondack Review*; *Barn Owl Review*; *Bat City Review*; *Boiler Magazine*; *Colorado Review*; *Devil's Lake*; *DIAGRAM*; *Drunken Boat*; the *Fiddleback*; *Gazing Grain Press*; *Greying Ghost Pamphlet Series*; *Guernica*; *iARTistas*; *InDigest Magazine*; the *Journal*; *La Petite Zine*; the *Leveler*; *Linebreak*; *No, Dear*; *Paperbag Magazine*; the *Paris-American*; *Phantom Limb*; *Pinwheel*; Poetry Society of America *In Their Own Words*; *Quotidian Bee*; *Sink Review*; *Sixth Finch*; *smoking glue gun*; *Spinning Jenny*; *Stoked*; *Thrush*; *Tin House*; *Two Serious Ladies*; *Vinyl Poetry*; *West Branch*.

Some of the poems in *Swan Feast* appear in the chapbook *Conversation with the Stone Wife*, published by Bloof Books in 2014. Five of the poems appear in the anthology *Electric Gurlesque* published by Saturnalia Books.

The title of the poem "Imprecation" was a word deliciously introduced to me by the poet Dawn Marie Knopf, who blew me away for years with her own incredible poem of the same name.

Thank you so much to the following brilliant folks who have stewarded me with ideas, advice, support, wine, and love during the making of *Swan Feast*: Dolan Morgan, Shanna Compton, Mark Cugini, Amy Brinker, Lily Lamboy, Marlo Starr, Molly Rose Quinn, Roxy Palmer, Matt McNamara, Meghann Plummer, Monica McClure, Jay Demetillo, Morgan Parker, Justin Boening, Allyson Paty, Danniel Schoonebeek, Tom Oristaglio, Sarah V. Schweig, Tyler Gobble, Sasha Fletcher, Siena Oristaglio, Timothy Donnelly, Lucie Brock-Broido, Josh Bell, Julie Carr, Feng Sun Chen, Cynthia Arrieu-King, Anna Moschovakis, Monica Ferrell, Danielle Pafunda, Julia Guez, Jay Deshpande, Nicole Rogers, Liz Clark Wessel, Dan Rogers, Emily Raw, Joe DeLuca, Sean H. Doyle, Tyler Weston, Mike Lala, Matthew Zingg, Ricky Maldonado, Soren Stockman, Carson Donnelly, Alex Morris, Alexandra Zelman-Doring, Jesse Garces Kiley, Shireen Madon, Dai George, Jameson Fitzpatrick, Keegan Lester, Melissa Broder, Skyler Balbus, Nina Puro, Julie Marie Wade, Carrie Lorig, Lynn Melnick, Leora Fridman, Joanna C. Valente, and of course, my family—David, Jean, Brandon, and Jordan Eilbert.

About the Author

Photo by Emily Raw

Natalie Eilbert is the author of two chapbooks, *Conversation with the Stone Wife* (Bloof Books, 2014) and *And I Shall Again Be Virtuous* (Big Lucks Books, 2014). Her work has appeared in the *New Yorker*, *Tin House*, the *Kenyon Review*, *Poem-a-Day* by the Academy of American Poets, *Guernica*, and many other journals. She is the founding editor of the *Atlas Review*. *Swan Feast* is her first poetry collection.

Praise for *Swan Feast*

Natalie Eilbert's powerful first book is a twenty-first century hymn to the Venus of Willendorf, a 30,000-year-old figurine whose ample body is a protest against all that seeks to diminish us. Like Plath of "Lady Lazarus," Eilbert speaks with unbridled but precise rage; in lines of propulsive music she takes female self-loathing head on and reveals it for what it is, pervasive, invasive, and invented, like a city that threatens to divest us of our human/animal body. Deeply resistant, these poems get the body back, feeding it, adoring it, finally marrying it, with flamboyance, flare and love. This is the voice of contemporary feminism, brazen, smart, unafraid, and desirous of nothing less than life. —Julie Carr

Natalie Eilbert uses an immense attention—in sentences filigreed and permissive—to show how the sexuality of the real and imagined Venus de Willendorf lives in our pulses, is our pulse, our Texas, our asses on the hood of a car in a trailer park. Every scrap that's flashed into this poet's mind transmutes into an icon for the flesh and the chaotic negotiation of one's desires. Few people can represent such vital, teeming complexity with such bridled rage. Plath stands in the recent past of this voice; Venus de Willendorf becomes a force within it you cannot imagine. Eilbert, standing so near to us, flinches at nothing. —Cynthia Arrieu-King

"There is no document of civilization that isn't also its ruins." Swan Feast is the banquet of a fallen goddess, told through the trance of an autobiographical duckling girl. The transforming voice is visionary. She connects the discovery of the Venus of Willendorf to the discovery of oil in the Middle East, implicating imperial industrialism to the passing away of Venus into faded memory and historical anorexia. Empire is the tomb of the goddess. To excavate is a "hilarious privilege," and its anachronism borrows illumination from darkness. The duckling is resurrecting ancient powers whose excavation ride on rage, grief, a woman's paradoxically empowered desperation which finds solidity in disappearance. In the wake of suffering, we may remember ourselves. Out of ruin, an alien star rises. —Feng Sun Chen

Time, and the world, want the body, and are coming for it. Natalie Eilbert tears the body down, and makes time and the world go looking for something else to want. Politically charged, performing a gnosticism of our human physiology, and impressionistic like a train, Swan Feast is both a book of poems and a preemptive strike. —Josh Bell

Eilbert dedicates herself completely to an enactment of history that is also an actual relationship to it / to herself / to a sick Anthropocene. *Swan Feast* is a violent autobiography, a girlface bleaching out of the headdress that adorns her / that feeds on her, a text that is both body / corpse, a speaking that acknowledges civilization / dissolves civilization into stone killing / into a stone that can kill the temple, a bursting / riot of mud / form / sculpture. I trust / it utters I trust / *N* utterly. —*Entropy*, Carrie Lorig

[Eilbert] will eat her words, of course, many times. She will "fork [her] failures until tender." That fricative again, harsh but necessary. She will become the swan meat that is "swallowed down with gold, gold soda." She will "grow into a small thing," the ultimate paradox. But she will know this is happening, and she will name it as it happens, and the Venus of Willendorf will write her a letter of fraught, feminist encouragement.

—*The Rumpus*, Julie Marie Wade

Eilbert is a remarkably deft poet. Her skill with form, along with the music of her words, lends a beauty to the book that scrapes against the sometimes difficult or raw language. —*Luna Luna Magazine*, Lynn Melnick

In her first poetry collection, *Swan Feast*, Natalie Eilbert does fascinating things with the embodied and re-bodied victim. Maybe Eilbert's poems are a hopeful, escaping version of Sisyphus because they stand right in the way of their boulders. They see those boulders coming and they stand in their way.

—*Avidly, Los Angeles Review of Books*, Leora Fridman

CPSIA information can be obtained
at www.ICGtesting.com
Printed in the USA
BVOW08s2201081216
469683BV00008B/9/P